How to
KILL YOUR COMPANY

50 Ways You're Bleeding Your
Organization and Damaging Your Career

Ken Kirsh

www.KillYourCompany.com

iUniverse, Inc.
Bloomington

How To Kill Your Company
50 Ways You're Bleeding Your Organization
and Damaging Your Career

iUniverse books may be ordered through booksellers or by contacting:

iUniverse
1663 Liberty Drive
Bloomington, IN 47403
www.iuniverse.com
1-800-Authors (1-800-288-4677)

ISBN: 978-1-4759-0526-7 (sc)
ISBN: 978-1-4759-0527-4 (e)
ISBN: 978-1-4759-0528-1 (dj)

Printed in the United States of America

iUniverse rev. date: 8/17/2012

WARNING

No formulas, paradigms, charts, matrices, acronyms, or secrets
were used in the making of this book.

To David

Learn from your mistakes and you'll get there easier.

Learn from others' mistakes and you'll get there faster.

"Everyone thinks of changing the world,

but no one thinks of changing himself."

— Leo Tolstoy

CONTENTS

III. With Your Habits   33

NOW WHAT?   55

WHAT'S AT STAKE?

What This Book Will Do for You

Left unchecked, the stark truths exposed in *How to Kill Your Company* will undermine your company's profitability and lead to your great undoing—along with your company's image and stock price. You will no doubt recognize friends, associates, and high-level executives—some of them public figures—throughout these pages.

The bigger questions are: Will you recognize yourself and what will you do about it? It's not too late...probably.

Here's what *How to Kill Your Company* will do for you, simply and directly:

o Expose what you're doing wrong

o Help you become immediately more productive

o Improve the odds of success for you and your organization

Who Should Read It

Everyone who wants to get ahead, help his or her company succeed, and do the right thing. If you're part of the C-suite and think you're immune from these issues, think again. It's not your vision or intellect that will get you into trouble; it's how you apply those very strengths, as well as your work style.

Whatever your role in the company, these traits and issues apply to all positions—up one side of the corporate ladder and down the other. That includes you.

This book is a quick read and not one of those you put aside after reading just a few chapters. I dare you not to finish it.

Why You Should Believe Me

With 25 years of experience as a communications consultant and business meeting producer, I've witnessed firsthand the problems organizations have getting the most out of their employees and management across the board. Not just training and motivating but truly maximizing the productivity and engagement of their most precious commodity: *human capital.* Otherwise known as you.

Given my role and experience, I've also worked with many of the world's top business speakers and authors. Like you, I've heard and read much of the conventional wisdom about what we should be doing. Problem is, *un*conventional wisdom is just as useful but in shorter supply. In other words, it's equally instructive to consider what you should not be doing; we'll call these *intrusions.*

I wrote this book by collecting and analyzing counterproductive behaviors I have observed people in all positions and industries repeatedly exhibit, shining a light on the most common among them. You'll see what I mean in just the first few pages. And I'm sorry to say that you'll see yourself in many of these chapters.

It's The Truth

If you're looking for hardcore evidence, research data, and statistics, you will be disappointed. People are not rats, generally speaking, and cannot be observed in adequately controlled workplace conditions to bear out my perceptions and commentary using traditional methods.

That said, I'm confident you will find my empirical study, if you will, reflects reality and the irrefutable truth. In fact, I'm willing to bet the only appreciable difference between your sense of things and mine is that I am so utterly fascinated by these behaviors that I am compelled to stick our collective faces in it. Someone has to tell you the truth and it may as well be me.

Making the Most of This Exploration

There are more moving parts in your life—more things competing for your time—than ever before, and it will continue this way. Your time is your most precious commodity; you never seem to have enough of it. That's why I spent a long time making this book short. You can read it in an hour or so, yet the revelations will resonate for years.

Listed in the contents are 50 things you're doing wrong to one extent or another. They are loosely organized into three categories to make it easier to process and explore; they are not listed in order of priority or any other parameter.

Just as you wouldn't look in the mirror all day but rather from time to time, you can look into these intrusions individually or in groups as time permits. But whether you go straight through from start to finish or in sections, each chapter will reflect the truth, reveal what you're doing wrong, and show why you should contemplate changing the way you think and act.

Most importantly, take note of the two boxes at the end of each topic and assess yourself truthfully, instinctively, without overthinking your answer. Keep track of your answers; they will become what you need to work on, as we'll discuss at the end of this book and self-assessment.

Retraining Your Instincts

None of the concepts in this book approach brain surgery—though you will ultimately be responsible for making changes to your brain, to the way you think. Call it *mind surgery*.

You need to rethink and retrain many of your instincts because they are wrong. When you consider how many people work at any given organization without reaching their potential, it becomes clear: You're not just killing your own chances of getting ahead, you're also killing your company.

The End Game

I can't solve your problems; that's your job. But I can promise to illuminate, to make you feel uncomfortable, and to point you in the right direction. It's time for you to take that long, hard look in the mirror and face up to what you should *not* be doing.

Keep in mind the goal is not to be without guilt. The goal is to isolate your weaknesses, create a baseline for change, and begin retraining your instincts so you can better serve yourself and your company or association. No matter where you are on the totem pole, the job you save will be your own.

I. PERSONALITY

Chapter 1   Set A Bad Example

You arrive late to your own meetings.

You change your mind incessantly.

You create urgent deadlines when they're just not necessary.

Your attire, language, and disposition are inappropriate.

And so on.

You don't need to run a company or lead a division or region to set an example. You have coworkers, and believe it or not, they notice you. They observe your work ethic, how you conduct yourself, and how you relate to others.

No matter how hidden among your peers you think you are, people get you—they're aware of your conduct—and it impacts them. If you do lead or manage others, the example you set is all the more important.

Keep in mind that setting the right example extends beyond your company's four walls. How you act with suppliers, competitors, partners, and the general public makes a difference too.

Come on, now. Get it together.

You Set a Bad Example   ❐ Guilty   ❐ Not Guilty

Chapter 2   Be Too Controlling

Sorry, this one hurts, I know. You're probably accused of this more than you like and more than is warranted. Thing is, taking control is essential to your company's growth and success. The other thing is, you take it too far. Where do you draw the line?

Deciding how much control to take isn't always easy. Just how far to go with people and situations depends on the circumstances.

That said…

You micromanage.

You lack trust in others.

You think you're the most capable.

You refuse to let go.

You impose your will too much and too often.

They say you can never be too thin or too rich. Perhaps. But your instinct to seize as much control as possible is definitely too much of a good thing, like overexposure to the sun or relying too much on one club. There's a time and place to control, such that you'll otherwise jam the mechanism, a surefire way to bleed your organization and damage your career.

I realize this is a tough one. I'm just saying think about it. Then change.

You're Too Controlling   ❐ Guilty   ❐ Not Guilty

Chapter 3   Put Your Ego In The Way

You're kidding, right? You don't see this? Everyone else does... *every*one.

Not only does pride goeth before a fall, it wreaks havoc on the way down—throughout the offices, cubicles, elevators, cafeterias, and conference rooms of Corporate America. Egos like yours are littering these places, and it's polluting your company.

I'm not concerned here with the pride you feel from doing a good job or ego as it relates to self-esteem. Those are good things. I'm talking about your ego when it drives bad decisions and puts people off, all because of your childlike need for attention, approval, and self-gratification.

I'm not finished.

You cut people off, talk down to them, and look at your watch while they're talking. You're abrasive, insensitive, short. You think your ideas are always better, take too long to get back to people, and tell them "I told you so" when you never told them anything. You reply to emails when it's convenient for you and, even then, only respond to part of it. You're frequently late, say inappropriate things, and people have a hard time challenging or advising you—much less reporting to you—because you know so much. You're just so important.

Not you? If you're guilty of even one of these things, you're putting people off and hurting the team. More than likely, it can be traced to your ego.

Now, where was I? Oh, yeah, you let your ego get in the way. Stop that.

Your Ego is in the Way   ❏ Guilty   ❏ Not Guilty

Chapter 4 Hog All The Credit

Why do you take credit for other people's ideas and efforts?

This is perhaps one of the lowest things you can do. It's not just lame—it's stupid. Everyone knows what's going on. You will not get away with it. Maybe you should try coming up with ideas of your own.

When you shine a light on others' good work, it reflects back on you. Crediting others is the stuff of corporate karma. When you point out the good that someone else does, whether you're his or her boss or not, the morale of everyone around you improves, and your social stock rises. Plus, your company prospers. It can't be measured directly or financially, but be assured that it does.

Try coming up with ideas and successes of your own. In any case, don't act like something is your idea when it's not. Don't take the credit; give it where it's due. It will actually come back to you.

Remember, honesty is always an alternative.

You Hog All the Credit   ❐ Guilty   ❐ Not Guilty

Chapter 5   Be Afraid Of Commitment

It's tempting to suggest that any one of the failings included here is the most common one. Such is the case with commitment.

The percentages overwhelmingly point to this as one of the greatest reasons people and companies fail. Not because they don't have a good product or service, or good people in place, but because they can't—or don't—see things through all the way.

You've heard that it's always darkest before the dawn, that when the going gets tough, the tough get going, and so on. The key point here is that you will fall short of your greatest possible success if you are not fully vested and committed.

This means approaching every task with 100% effort. Completely. All the way through. *All* the way.

If you want to outrun a bear, I don't recommend being kind of committed to running away.

If the bear happens to be your boss, being completely prepared, not partially, is always the right choice.

It's the same with your company. Neither of you can afford to leave anything on the table.

Commitment is the overarching quality that determines how far you will go because it defines how far you are *willing* to go.

You're Afraid of Commitment   ❐ Guilty   ❐ Not Guilty

Chapter 6   Allow Your Attention Span To Shrink

Your attention span is shrinking faster than a cheap cotton T-shirt. Everyone jokes about it—and laughs because it's the truth, and the truth is funny. Guess what. It's not funny. And it's killing your company.

I'm not saying you're clinically ADD or that you need medication. But I am saying you may have spent too much time watching music videos.

If you're under 35, you never had a chance; every movie, video game, and television commercial is now edited to within an inch of its life.

The good news, whatever your age, is that you've gotten better at processing information faster. This multitasking back and forth enables you to be more productive and efficient—provided you're not glossing over things or dropping important information in the cracks along the way.

Hopefully, you have been training your mind to function more digitally, the way younger generations have already grown up, so you can carry the ball with agility, turning on a dime rather than running in straight lines.

But the bigger point here is that while your attention span is shrinking, you can still strike the right balance between speed and focus based on the urgency and outcomes being sought for the task at hand. In other words, you must adopt a situational focus if you can't stay there for long periods of time.

Keep ignoring this balance at your own peril—and that of your company.

Your Attention Span is Shrinking   ❏ Guilty   ❏ Not Guilty

Chapter 7   Be A Hypocrite

You project one thing publicly and act based on another privately.

You say one thing to your colleagues and do another.

You pretend to believe one thing while actually believing something else.

You talk the talk but don't walk the walk.

These are all different from asking someone how he or she is doing even if you don't really care; such niceties are perfectly acceptable white lies of sorts that grease the wheels of any organization, even a family.

But when your actions belie your words, and you're trying to avoid being found out, you are fooling no one. Your attempts at concealing your two-faced talk and duplicitous actions will catch up with you sooner than you think. And it only takes a single act of hypocrisy to earn such a label.

Come on. Do you really believe such juvenile, deceitful behavior will serve you in the workplace? Get real. And while you're at it, get honest.

You're a Hypocrite   ❑ Guilty   ❑ Not Guilty

Chapter 8   Lack Confidence

Just because someone is courageous doesn't mean they're not afraid or insecure at times. Even the greatest of leaders and competitors have respect for their opponents and for circumstances that can impact their chances of victory or survival.

But it's hard to succeed without confidence, whatever the odds. Indeed, without it, virtually nothing great happens—including long term profit growth. Your team, division, region, company and even you are destined to fall short due to your lack of it.

When you're fearful, desperate, or insecure, you tend to either withdraw or go unnoticed, or conversely, blame, freak out, and condescend to others. Whether you are you are managing yourself or a group, confidence will improve morale and take you farther. It costs nothing, your company feeds off it, and it's all in your head.

In sports, confidence often makes the difference between being out and safe, getting the first down and falling short, sinking a putt and missing by inches. In business, it's what gets you one more increment of success, however you measure it: time, money, image, and so on.

You should be identifying things you can be confident about and creating ways to improve your lack of it as relates to others and to outcomes. You don't want to infect people with negativity but a confidence virus is something else entirely…it's all good.

You Lack Confidence   ❒ Guilty   ❒ Not Guilty

Chapter 9   Act Or Feel Entitled

Either way, it's wrong, and I'll tell you why: The world owes you nothing.

That's it. Were you expecting more?

Younger people are accused of this more often—and deservedly so. They often consider their problems big and their work hard, compared to real problems and extra hard work. Some were brought up in a more coddled fashion. They are naïve, if well-meaning. I've been there. How about you?

If you're under 40 and feel entitled, get over it. You deserve nothing; life is tough, then gets tougher, then you die, so make the most of it.

If you're over 40 and entitled, you have even bigger problems. Not only are you acting in a self-defeating manner, but you've also spent a long time not learning this valuable lesson. And it applies to life as much as business.

If you act entitled, people will be put off. If you feel entitled, your future will be put off. Thinking the world or anyone in it owes you something is negative programming and, quite simply, wrong. It just doesn't work that way.

You Act or Feel Entitled   ❏ Guilty   ❏ Not Guilty

Chapter 10 Don't Be Yourself

When you conceal who you really are and what you really think, three things happen.

First, once people find out who you really are, they will no longer trust you. This will last a long time. Forever, actually. And they *will* find out.

Second, people who perceived you as disingenuous in the first place will be validated. Do I need to explain why this is a bad thing?

Third, whether or not you're aware you're being duplicitous, or you're simply cut off from yourself, you are living a lie. And when your actions are incongruent with your values and beliefs, sooner or later, you will fall. This will extend to your personal life.

Duplicity is the sister of hypocrisy; they are evil twins, cracks in your personal foundation that inevitably spread to that of your company. You need to know who you are, what you think and stand for, and reflect those truths in your words and actions.

Yes, there's a balance. You don't need to offend people or put yourself at risk by sharing too much. And maybe there are a few things about yourself that you should hide.

But in general, pretending to be something you're not—concealing things that bear mentioning, being disingenuous, acting inconsistent with your core principles—will not only kill your reputation and your company but your hopes of advancement. Promise.

You're Not Yourself   ❐ Guilty   ❐ Not Guilty

Chapter 11 Collect A Paycheck

Face it. You're just going through the motions. You don't really show up. You phone it in like some old dinner theater hack who's bitter, bored, broken—or "D," all of the above.

Maybe your company doesn't notice you're phoning it in, so it's okay. Really? Trust me, you stand out worse than a bad mime. Just because you're physically at your workplace doesn't mean you're performing well or even doing your job.

You can't just move things around, talk to a few people, reply to some emails, and attend a few meetings. Your company doesn't need you to do a good job; it needs you to do a *great* one. And it's not easily fooled. Too often, you're faking it—and everyone can tell.

Trust me, you will be found out. Better to cop to it now than be exposed for the hack you are later. You are bleeding your organization and damaging your career. Think that's too dramatic? Think again.

Lack of engagement is a killer in the workplace and out. Even if you don't go the extra mile, at least go the miles your company is paying you to go. In other words, do your damn job.

You're Collecting a Paycheck   ❏ Guilty ❏ Not Guilty

Chapter 12 Be Ignorant And Apathetic

You're apathy's showing. So is your ignorance. Unfortunately, everyone sees it but you. But you don't know, and you don't care.

While these two traits function independently, they frequently trigger one another, hence the pairing. In fact, if bad traits are killers, these are the ninja assassins. They sneak up on you and, before you know it, it's too late. They will destroy not only your company but also your personal potential.

In the corporate arena, ignorance is anything but bliss. There is always a great deal for you to know: policies, procedures, philosophies, products, services, priorities, your place, your boss's preferences, your coworkers' styles, the competition, and so on, not to mention your job—inside out. You even have to know something about your next job; otherwise, why should you be promoted to it?

And what of apathy?

Well, you'd better care. It just might be the single greatest unseen killer of raises and promotions there is. You can't hide apathy. It affects others—and not in a good way. You need to recognize the moment before you don't care anymore, then retool and recharge. Treat it like burnout because it's the last stage before that actually happens.

There is no substitute for knowing and caring as much as possible across the board. Here again, the job you save will be your own.

You're Ignorant and Apathetic   ❏ Guilty ❏ Not Guilty

Chapter 13 Be Too Complacent

Everything's fine.

Really?

You've been in the same position for years.

You're satisfied doing adequate work.

You're happy with the status quo.

Guess what. None of these are good for you—or your company. Believe it or not, your organization actually feeds on change. And part of that change is you climbing the corporate ladder, broadening your horizons, pushing yourself and shaking things up, so the company's resources, processes and output are optimized.

Business moves and changes in real time, not tomorrow or even an hour from now. There's a good chance what was great this morning will suck this afternoon.

On a broader scale, some organizations are proactive about moving people around. Some are not. If yours is the latter, you need to reevaluate your position every so often and make some noise.

If you keep up, all right then. If you keep a step ahead, even better. But if you remain complacent, your work and company will suffer, and you will be up jobless creek without a reference.

When you get complacent, you feel its effects.

When you fail to recognize it, your *company* feels it.

When you fail do something about it, your *customers* feel it.

You're Too Complacent ❏ Guilty ❏ Not Guilty

Chapter 14 Resist Change And Opportunity

You dislike change and seek to avoid it. Big mistake. You overlook opportunity even when it's right in front of you. Bigger mistake.

Few things stay the same—and that's fine. When you stop changing, you stop evolving. When you stop evolving, you're less useful and interesting to everyone around you. This includes your company, lest you forget our theme here. Resisting change kills opportunity; they are inextricably linked.

Be slow to embrace new ideas, methods, and policies, and you risk losing your job. The established way of doing things is ideal only until someone creates a better one. You need to make new approaches work for you not against, see the upside not the down, and recognize that initiating change is better than having it imposed on you.

Opportunity is hidden as often as it is obvious. It rarely announces itself in the form of benefit or advantage; uncovering that is your job.

Whether targeted or sweeping, companies reorganize more fully and frequently than ever before. This is done to be more efficient, to save money in the long run, to be competitive—in short, to survive—not as fodder for you to complain. The speed and frequency of change will not slow or reverse but accelerate.

Resist change and opportunity, and you will fall behind. As with many of the issues here, you may be as guilty of this in your personal life as you are professionally.

You Resist Change and Opportunity   ❐ Guilty ❐ Not Guilty

Chapter 15 Be Surprised By The Expected

You project and anticipate with clarity and precision. You're smart, thoughtful, incisive, and generally know what to expect from people and situations—and you are usually right. So, why is it you're surprised when someone reacts or behaves just as you would expect?

Your boss makes the misguided decision you predicted.

The division head promotes his friend over a better candidate.

Progress stalls due to infighting and competing interests.

You're appalled but not surprised, yet you act that way, wasting time fixated on outcomes you predicted—rather than considering your insight a gift and how you can make it work for you.

Hopefully, you manage expectations well in general—yours and those of your boss, colleagues, clients, and others.

But this counterproductive thinking creeps up on you insidiously, like a swarm of no-see-ums. Better to turn your brain off and your idiot repellent on.

Whether the conversation is in your head or with a coworker, don't get caught up in this loop. Stop shaking your head in wonder when something turns out exactly how you would have guessed in the first place. You need to focus on the important thing: real surprises.

You're Surprised by the Expected ☐ Guilty ☐ Not Guilty

Chapter 16 Look For Secrets And Shortcuts

You spend more time looking for ways around things than it takes to complete them. You're too lazy and misguided to realize that you're lazy and misguided—and it's killing your company.

Want to know the secret to getting any task accomplished—simple or complex—in the shortest possible time?

Do your job.

Not much of a secret, is it? That's because there are no secrets. If there were, *Secrets and Shortcuts* would be the name of this book.

There are no secrets or shortcuts. And if there is a magic bullet, it's you...*you* are the magic bullet.

Stop looking for ways around things. Start helping others with their jobs. If you are deficient in some way, work on improving yourself and leverage your relationships to get what you need. Work hard. Work smart. Use your head. Use other people's heads.

Getting around the bases quickly is important, but it means nothing if you fail to tag one of them.

You Look for Secrets and Shortcuts   ❐ Guilty ❐ Not Guilty

Chapter 17 Spread Negative Waves

That'll never work.

We've never done it that way.

That sounds complicated.

I'm sure we can't agree to that.

This new process stinks.

My boss is a jerk.

This place makes me sick.

Shut up already. (That's not another example—I'm talking to you.)

Look, I know it's not easy to maintain a positive attitude 100% of the time. The pressures of life and work are great. The moving parts are many, and the stress never stops.

That said, you have to be positive. If you can't, just don't be negative. If you feel a moment of negativity coming on, head for the nearest broom closet or take a walk. Just keep away from the one thing you can infect with such talk—everyone else. The only people who enjoy listening to others complain are other complainers. Guess what. It's toxic and, yes, it's killing your company.

If you feel frustrated, channel it in a productive way or shut up. Otherwise, you'll earn a reputation that, I assure you, you don't want. No one is saying you have to be Mr. or Ms. Positive all the time. There are certainly times to vent and to question. But make a habit of shooting down others and you'll bleed all the way to your next job interview.

You Spread Negative Waves   ☐ Guilty ☐ Not Guilty

II. RELATIONSHIPS

Chapter 18 Lack Trust, Respect, And Empathy

You consider other people's thoughts, feelings, and ambitions—when it's convenient for you. You are otherwise disrespectful, unthinking, and distrusting. If a video game were created about interpersonal disaster, you'd be its chief designer.

If you took a moment to consider how your actions and decisions affect your boss, subordinates, peers, customers, and others, you would actually enhance your position and your organization's well-being.

Stop wondering why you lack the respect of others. Stop wondering why people keep secrets from you. Stop wondering why no one seems to consider your point of view.

Start thinking about others and all those concerns will go away. All you have to do to gain the trust, respect, and empathy of others is to give it. Pretty simple, isn't it?

I've grouped these three traits because they often travel together. But they go it alone as well. Look for them, together and separately; they live in the subtext of many other chapters here.

Don't get me wrong: Skepticism and self-centered behavior have their place and are not unhealthy in and of themselves. They are crucial to upward mobility. Start thinking of them as nice places to visit, but you wouldn't want to live there.

You Lack Trust, Respect, and Empathy ❒ Guilty ❒ Not Guilty

Chapter 19 Don't Compromise

Great leaders understand compromise. In fact, all great parents, athletes, lawyers, artists, teachers, politicians, doctors, business people—in short, everyone knows they have to make sacrifices and compromises to get what they want.

Except you. You're different. You don't have to compromise.

You also don't have to succeed.

I'm here to tell you that you can't have it all. So, whatever it is you're looking for—project approval, better terms, a later deadline, time off, more money—get as much as you can and get out. Maybe come back later, leaving and returning as part of a negotiating strategy.

Of course, you shouldn't leave anything on the table that you have the ability to get. But you need to break your habit and lose the reputation you have for not giving in and having everything your way. Besides, the other guy may have a point—one that might even help you in the long run.

You Don't Compromise   ❏ Guilty ❏ Not Guilty

Chapter 20 Build And Protect Silos

Your instinct is to control and protect. You share only what comes back to you in income, stature, security, promotions, or more control and influence.

The company is not selfish. You are.

Your company wants you to succeed, but it needs to grow. And it feeds on the very communication you block and overmanage.

You must find the common ground between your self-interests and other departments/divisions to meet your company's needs. Your company is bigger and more important to you than you realize.

I can't believe I even have to explain this to you, but apparently you're not alone; it's one of the most common problems I've observed. This doesn't mean you should feel better because so many people are guilty of this offense. On the contrary, it means you need to differentiate yourself as someone who understands how much more trusting, insightful, and open you ought to be.

No one is threatening your job. Your company needs and wants you to be in control and in charge of your area. It just wants you to share what others in your organization need from you. The company's left hand needs to know what its right hand is doing; if it doesn't, it will confuse itself, then confuse its customers, then lose money.

Have confidence that this communication will come back to you in even greater returns.

You Build and Protect Silos ☐ Guilty ☐ Not Guilty

Chapter 21 Be Too Political

Your job requires you to be political.

You must angle for your next promotion, project, raise, or bonus.

You must also navigate waters made murky by others—and engage or circumvent people to assist you or approve your projects.

But...

You're being too political. You are obstructing the natural flow of information, process, and interaction that your company requires.

If you're politicking for a subordinate or coworker, good for you. Politics should be about the greater good—not just as it relates to you.

While some people are not politically assertive enough, the bigger problem I've observed is that most are too political. For your company's sake, you need to strike the right balance; more often than not, this means toning it down a bit, not up.

If you're guilty of this behavior, you know exactly what I'm talking about. If you're not, don't get too comfortable. Chances are you're more than a little guilty of what comes next.

You're Too Political   ❏ Guilty ❏ Not Guilty

Chapter 22 Cut Yourself Off

Whether it's the door to your office or your mind that's closed, you can't share or engage others—or encourage those around you to do the same—under such conditions.

Shutting your door literally and figuratively shuts out the flow of information, ideas, and energy to you and from you, and with it, your chance at greater success and impact.

You are creating a communication breakdown similar to building and protecting silos. However, in this case, the breakdown is more personal: You're cutting yourself off, not just your team.

This flow, in and out of your office and your mind, is critical to your company's growth. It's what helps make things happen, get better, create positive outcomes.

Consider the musician or improv comic whose mindset is always "yes and." They are 360 degrees open because they know the best way to make something better is to accept what they see and hear, then build on it. You need to emulate that mindset.

You also need to create an atmosphere of "the door is always open". Besides, if you keep your door shut, how can anyone bring you an alternative solution or a useful idea you can build on?

Need a minute of privacy or solitude? Fine. Shut the door to your office or put on your headphones. Otherwise, if someone closes the door on the way in, make sure they leave it open on the way out. If you've cut yourself off, consider opening up and finding ways to stay connected beyond emails, conference calls, and virtual meetings.

You need to think of your mind as the doorway to success, and keep it open all the time.

You Cut Yourself Off ❏ Guilty ❏ Not Guilty

Chapter 23 Trust Your Advisor

There's one trap many astute people—generals and foot soldiers alike—fall into. It's as dangerous as any issue I've addressed—not just in and of itself but because it's insidious and can eventually lead to a war of sorts. It's a killer, all right. Big time.

You know that team you have in place? The group you personally assembled? That go-to person whose advice you value so highly?

Run, don't walk. They're steering you into hostile territory.

Still not getting it? You are listening to the wrong voices, getting advice from the wrong people, and trusting the wrong input. Even if they mean well, they are infecting your mind with bad information, advice, or solutions.

You must be hyper-vigilant to avoid this land mine. You cannot see it, touch it, or smell it. Indeed, it's often camouflaged in the guise of well-meaning, well-delivered, well-thought-out input.

But it is wrong. Dead wrong. You need another way to assess and verify this person or group's battle plan...or you will find yourself on the battlefield with the right gun and the wrong ammunition.

This one really worries me because it's very hard to see, and it's even harder to believe. If I knew a surefire way to help you detect bad advice or to avoid being manipulated, I would tell you. But you need to know who is guiding you right, and who is guiding you right into enemy hands.

Your Trusted Advisor Can't Be ☐ Guilty ☐ Not Guilty

Chapter 24 Gossip Too Much

Who doesn't like to gossip?

The short answer is: dedicated and productive workers who keep their noses to the grindstone.

That said, conversation about coworkers is natural and can even provide valuable insights and foster camaraderie. If you're in politics, management, reporting, law enforcement, or real estate, for example, your livelihood actually depends in part on mining gossip.

Talking about coworkers to help navigate workplace dynamics can also be very useful.

But small-minded dialogue is counterproductive and says more about you than the people you're discussing. If you really need to gossip, do it on your own time and move on. Or better yet, leave it to the professionals; there are plenty of magazines and online outlets for that stuff. Or save it for your hairstylist.

Gossiping about others has been around since the first caveman spoke ill of the second. But its usefulness is situational; while everyone does it to some extent, we can use our brains to pick low-hanging fruit or to reach for bigger, smarter ideas.

If you don't distinguish between gossip that's useful and that which is petty, you'll fall short—and into the trap.

You Gossip Too Much ☐ Guilty ☐ Not Guilty

Chapter 25 Bleed Suppliers

Why do you treat suppliers like second-class citizens? Are you on a power trip or just mean and misguided? Aren't the suppliers that are charging you also fueling you?

Your company needs you to get the best price. Sometimes that means the least expensive; sometimes it means the best value.

Your company needs you to get the best service. This can mean speed, flexibility, safety, attitude, and a host of other things.

Your company needs you to get the best quality. Depending on your business and the situation, this can mean demanding perfection or tolerating passable.

It's your job to understand when to apply what parameters, and to treat suppliers with candor and the same respect you want from them. Expense is half of the equation in business; savings go right to the bottom line. But you also depend on your suppliers, don't you?

Be straightforward about the bidding process, the reasons behind it, and the outcomes being sought. You can be demanding *and* respectful. Cut them if you must…but don't bleed them. The last thing your company needs is a serial killer.

You Bleed Suppliers   ❏ Guilty ❏ Not Guilty

Chapter 26 Matter More Than The Team

Team sports metaphors are rampant in business speeches, motivational videos, and those awful posters. And while they're incredibly tiresome and cliché, they're also incredibly relevant.

The individual can never grow, learn, succeed, or contribute as much when he is focused on himself as when he is serving the team. Just ask any coach or player at any level.

The irony is that if you're really self-centered, you will opt to serve the greater good because it will come back to you in the form of victory, pride, and tangible rewards. The best thing you can do for yourself is to do what's best for the team—your company. The top scorers in any sport will tell you that they got there on assists from others.

If you subscribe to the thinking there is no "I" in team, but there is "me," get over yourself. Even the greatest pitchers need competent fielders and a good offense to win (speaking of sports metaphors).

Next time you have the chance to take one for the team, take two. It won't hurt. It will help.

You Matter More Than the Team   ❐ Guilty ❐ Not Guilty

Chapter 27 Don't Know Your Audience

Maybe you just don't care enough. Either way, you're screwed. You'd probably suck as a therapist, but you're definitely not the communicator you could be. Why do you assume people are people—that they're all the same?

If you want to inspire or influence—whether you're speaking to one person or thousands—never assume that what makes you tick is what makes them tick. You have to consider their demographic and psychographic profiles, age, background, gender, intelligence, culture, position, values, beliefs, and circumstances—in short, their frame of reference.

Speakers, politicians, and entertainers are masters at this. They research and/or intuit what makes their audiences feel, think, open up, and shut down. They consider what material will reach their audiences with the greatest impact, what will make them laugh, cry, think, act a certain way, tap their toes, whatever.

If you want to get through to your boss, subordinate, peer, or a group of people of any type or size, you must know how they think, what they question and value, how they intellectualize, their disposition, and what matters to them.

Whether it's to inform, instruct, inspire, or influence in a formal presentation or a casual chat in the hallway, you need to start thinking more about others instead of yourself.

Before you attempt to sell anyone on anything, grand or mundane, consider their perspective. It will make or break your ability to connect with them and, not incidentally, to do your job.

You Don't Know Your Audience ❏ Guilty ❏ Not Guilty

Chapter 28 Don't Belong There

You don't feel you belong—or worse, that's how others perceive you. Ever stop to think you may be working at the wrong company? This type of mismatch is one reason sports teams trade players, often to everyone's benefit.

Whether it's forced upon you or of your own volition, you owe it to yourself and your company to take stock every so often:

Are you performing with passion and to the best of your ability?

If not, is it because you're in the wrong place? Is the fit not right?

Is your relationship with your company healthy?

Would you and your company be better off with you somewhere else?

Your organization does not want to see you, let alone pay you, if you really should be working elsewhere. They'd rather see you go and replace you with someone who is right for the job, who fits better with their goals and culture.

If you belong, get to work. If you don't, get to work on your exit strategy.

You Don't Belong Here ☐ Guilty ☐ Not Guilty

Chapter 29 Win Battles Instead Of Wars

This is so cliché, yet it dominates your thinking, and you do nothing to stop it.

Guess who's at fault? Exactly.

Stop arguing already. There's a good chance you have something much bigger and more important to deal with in the long run.

You were taught this but failed to learn it. Isn't it one of the most basic principles in all of human interaction? Why then do you insist on winning every incidental point of every negotiation of every exchange?

Call it self-sabotage: You're in control, yet you undermine your relationships and the achievement of your end goals.

If you focus on solving problems, attempt to create win-win situations, and give a little ground, you will likely claim even more territory, move closer toward your goals, and enhance your stature.

Understand concession, cooperation, and collaboration, and add them to your skill set.

Some organizations do such a good job of bogging down negotiations and losing sight of the big picture, that any time there's a minor advance, let alone breakthrough, it makes the headlines. You should learn from them and from people you observe doing the same thing—and do the opposite.

If you continue to value winning over problem solving, it will cost you in the end, and your company will pay the price.

You Win Battles Instead of Wars   ❐ Guilty   ❐ Not Guilty

Chapter 30 Pass the Buck

You fail to take responsibility.

You pass things off on someone else.

You drop the ball and lack the fortitude to admit it.

You judge, disapprove, blame, and find fault in others.

Problem is, the fault is yours.

Whether you're the boss or not, you're frustrating everyone, and worse, you're shooting yourself in the foot.

News Flash: When you shirk accountability for your actions or pass the responsibility on to someone else (as opposed to delegating) people see you as a creep and a coward. Trust me. They won't say it to your face, but everyone will shake their heads when they hear your name.

Accountability as a term is overused, and as a quality, under exemplified. Understand that holding yourself accountable and going beyond what you are responsible for is the right choice; blaming others and passing the buck is the wrong one.

Any questions?

You Pass the Buck   ❐ Guilty ❐ Not Guilty

III. HABITS

Chapter 31 Suck At Delegating

You do too much yourself. Whatever the reason—you think it's faster, handled better by you, others are incompetent—you're wrong, and you need to delegate more.

What? It's because you don't have anyone to delegate to? That may be, in which case you have to be far more efficient. But think about it: You don't only delegate down, you also delegate up and sideways. Think, too, about whether the task is necessary in the first place. Sometimes you can delegate to the trash can.

Perhaps you're too controlling, lack trust in others, see it as a sign of weakness, or you're the micromanaging type. Or maybe you think you're the smartest guy in the room and therefore have to handle everything yourself. If that's the case, you're clearly not the smartest guy in the room; if you were, you'd realize how much you could accomplish by delegating more. Every problem can't be so important or idiosyncratic that only you can solve it.

And what of the opposite problem: You assign and hand over too much. This is another way to suck at delegating and says more about your indolence and/or lack of accountability, both of which we'll get to.

If you're all strengths and no weaknesses, you needn't finish this book, let alone this chapter; if not, why aren't you delegating those things others can do better than you? Even if they can't do a better job and their work is merely adequate, sometimes good enough is good enough.

In any of these cases, you're not only misusing your time, you're lying to yourself—the one person with whom you should be the most honest, plus you're probably alienating those around you.

Bottom line? You need to let go. Give it away. Focus on more important things.

You Suck at Delegating ☐ Guilty ☐ Not Guilty

Chapter 32 Underthink Things

You think getting something off your desk is more important than getting it off your desk right. Stop checking things off your list unless you've given them proper attention. Either you're in too much of a rush, or you're being lazy.

Could a little more contemplation better inform your next move?

Could one more conversation with someone improve your overall direction?

Do you read emails too quickly, failing to answer the sender's questions?

Do you consider the implications, consequences, and perceptions of your actions/decisions?

Is it really off your desk or will it just be coming back with more questions or another iteration you can't afford to iterate?

Call it being thoughtful. Call it due diligence. Would you like your doctor to underthink your diagnosis, your financial planner to underthink your investment plan, or your boss to underthink the merit of giving you a raise? Didn't think so.

You need to chill, slow down, and think for a minute...or two.

You Underthink Things   ❑ Guilty   ❑ Not Guilty

Chapter 33 Overthink Things

Want another surefire way to kill your company? Keep overthinking things. It's the inverse of underthinking.

Your job, among countless other things, is to strike the right balance between too much and not enough:

Big picture vs. details.

Deliberation vs. action.

People's feelings vs. the company's needs.

Reasonable research vs. enough already.

You need to determine the right amount of thought, attention, time, and action to give things.

Stop overthinking (and underthinking) and consider how important each item that crosses your desk/computer/inbox truly is, and the effects of rushing versus poring over them. We needn't dispute which is worse, but let me remind you that, unlike the planet, the business world rotates faster every day.

You cannot afford to wait. You cannot afford to rush. This is the paradox you must reconcile daily.

You Overthink Things ☐ Guilty ☐ Not Guilty

Chapter 34 Be On Too Many Conference Calls

This kind of waste is so pervasive and egregious that it deserves its own chapter. It's foolish and unconscionable. Stop initiating all but the most critical. Refuse to join any that are not, or limit your involvement by imposing shorter fuses on your availability. Try to get your topic up first so you can avoid 55 minutes of standing by inefficiently.

Since you're not really paying attention anyway, you are being counter-productive and forfeiting time you could be spending on more important things.

Sure, you can fake it, whether you're at home in your underwear, out grocery shopping, emailing away on another project, or texting someone else on the call about how lame it is. But don't think you're fooling anyone when you say "excuse me?" Everyone knows you weren't listening in the first place, ok? You're busted.

In your office or conference room, stop rustling papers near the microphone or better yet, just put it on mute until you have something relevant or valuable to say. Try to replace yourself on these calls and get notes from someone else.

If you are leading the meeting, do so with purpose, focus and the utmost regard for everyone's time. If you are a participant, provide real answers, advance core goals and outcomes. Otherwise, shut up or get off. Your organization is paying you to make the best use of your time, not squander it.

For every ten or so hours of conference call time you avoid, you get back an entire work day. Do the math, then do yourself a favor.

You're on Too Many Conference Calls   ❑ Guilty   ❑ Not Guilty

---

Chapter 35 Attend Too Many Meetings

This is closely related to too many conference calls—except that here you're doing it in person. Worse. Much worse. You can't multitask or pretend to be listening—fake this one, and you'll be the first one called on for input. Guaranteed.

Years ago, a few forward-thinking companies removed something from their conference rooms: chairs. The idea was to keep meetings short and productive. No one gets too comfortable, and things keep moving.

I'm not saying you shouldn't attend meetings or conference calls. I'm saying that you attend too many and stay too long. If your boss insists you attend, explain how the best place for you to be is somewhere else. If you're the boss, stop holding so many meetings or keeping people so long it feels like a hostage crisis.

If it can be handled offline—in an email, in the elevator, with a phone call, or by your assistant—don't bring it up in a meeting. Other people's time is as precious as yours. Killing your own is one thing—killing someone else's is quite another.

Bottom line, you don't belong in these meetings. Get out.

You Attend Too Many Meetings   ❏ Guilty   ❏ Not Guilty

Chapter 36 Give Up Too Soon Or Too Late

The tide was about to turn, but you already jumped ship. Of course, life is tough; it's tough for everybody. But good things take time, and great things take more time.

In life and in business, things veer off in unexpected directions and often take longer than planned. And sometimes, things look so bleak, so dark, that you can be fooled into thinking it's too late.

But it's not.

You know this. So, why do you give up?

You must build into your everyday strategy what you will do when obstacles arise. You know they're coming—so why are you surprised or unprepared? This means balancing patience and audacity and being more perceptive. It also means defining and updating deadlines for success and recognizing when it's too late to change course.

The corollary to giving up too soon is holding on too long, which is equally damaging. Either way, it's a judgment call. But you are the judge and must reach the right decision at the right time, in between giving up too soon or too late.

It's easier to tell when you've held on too long because that critical moment, the ideal time to bail or change course, has already transpired. You're in hindsight mode and can see the problem more clearly, like the street you should have turned on after you passed it.

But you need to see it in well in advance…or even just in time.

You Give Up too Soon or Too Late   ❑ Guilty ❑ Not Guilty

Chapter 37 Cut Corners

There's compromise, and there's cutting corners. One is part of daily living and entails measured thought. The other is a bad habit and just plain foolish.

Imagine the perfectly cut and shaped grass at a major league ballpark. Imagine how odd and unbalanced the field would look if corners were cut. Now imagine that field as the landscape of your career.

It's not that cutting corners is always wrong. It's that you must consider the consequences as well as the frequency and extent of the kind of cutting you do.

Indiscriminately slashing budgets, shortening lead times, assigning projects randomly, making hasty decisions, compromising on service or quality, skimping on training—these are all death sentences. But while you're the guilty one, it's your company who will serve the time, one way or another.

The fix for this one is simple. But you won't do it...unless you're different from most. All you need to do is to think it through. Consider the implications and likely outcomes of cutting any given corner. In many cases, it may not make any sense—or worse, it may come back to haunt you.

You Cut Corners   ❐ Guilty ❐ Not Guilty

Chapter 38 Misunderstand The Basics

A related problem to ignoring or misjudging balance is misunderstanding basic concepts. That is, you confuse methods of thought and misapply them. Examples:

You think adding money to a budget is contingency planning.

You emphasize deadlines at the expense of outcomes.

You confuse goal setting with strategy.

You equate successful negotiation with winning.

You try to be all things to all people.

You use email when you should call or discuss in person.

Nothing is as simple or as complicated as you think; many things are not clear cut. If you find this unsettling, congratulations—you're making progress. It's referred to as being comfortable with being uncomfortable. You cannot always be settled, complete, or completely ready.

Your company needs you to understand the basics, to think, interpret, react, and be thoughtfully proactive, rather than just forging ahead on auto-pilot. It's often necessary to take a step back in order to take a step forward, and to be clear about how you intend to approach something, basic as the task may be.

You Misunderstand the Basics   ❐ Guilty   ❐ Not Guilty

Chapter 39 Be Accountable Without Control

This one's scent is subtle—until it happens to you. Then you'll smell it well into the next quarter.

Accepting responsibility without control is something thousands of people do unwittingly every day. They are tasked, for example, with reducing costs or managing people or running a project. But (and this is the mother of all "buts") they do not have the final authority or decision-making power over the way to get there or what actually constitutes success, which is often a moving target.

Therefore, the finger can be pointed at you if and when it fails, to whatever extent, because you are accountable for its success even though the rules were written and changed by others.

Is this you? If not, it's the person in the office or cubicle next to yours. (It's you.) If you are not given the tools, authority, time, money, choice of team, etc. required to do the job properly, yet you are responsible for its successful outcome, why are you taking responsibility in the first place?

It's one thing to dig a hole with a spoon if you're not given a shovel. It's another thing to dig it in the same amount of time. Reality, control, authority—they are all fundamental to managing a project to success.

There may be times you simply will not have a choice in the matter, but you must fight hard, very hard, for the authority and control you need to make it happen. Accepting responsibility is a good thing; being accountable without control is quite another. You increase your odds of failure, and that can't be good for your company.

You're Accountable without Control   ❑ Guilty   ❑ Not Guilty

Chapter 40 Email Too Much

You flood other people's inboxes.

You're misunderstood more often than you think.

You're asking questions and not getting answers.

You're missing the opportunity to forge better relationships.

You need to do your share and cut down on emailing when it's unnecessary or when live communication is more appropriate. Think about how many emails you get that are too long, too confusing, or shouldn't have been sent to you in the first place. Now, think about how others perceive your emails.

Most of the time, emailing is fine, of course. Sometimes it's a good idea to email and then call. Get your point across and documented, then call to clarify or reinforce what you're looking to say or elicit from them.

It's not just trees we need to save; it's our eyes and our time. Do your share by cutting down. Stop forwarding emails for someone else to deal with unless that's the right response.

Also, how are we supposed to contact you promptly and directly if you don't include your phone numbers in your signature, from both your computer and smart phone? Whether or not your communications are ambiguous, misguided, or require immediate discussion, you are inconveniencing people, and worse, putting yourself and your company at a disadvantage.

And for cripes sake, pick up the phone once in a while.

You Email Too Much   ❐ Guilty   ❐ Not Guilty

Chapter 41 Put Your Reputation At Risk

It takes years to build a good reputation, a single action to destroy it. You've heard this before, so why aren't you protecting your image as you should?

A lie, transgression, overreaching act—in short, anything that undermines trust—can tarnish your image and therefore your reputation. Everything you do strengthens or weakens your character, which is essentially how people judge you.

Being predictable isn't all bad. When people see you as someone who delivers, who walks the walk, and is consistent, they come to rely on you. Think about it. You are, in effect, teaching people every day what to think about you.

Even if you want a reputation as something other than kind, reasonable, reliable, easygoing—whatever—you must protect that image fiercely in order to serve your goal and your company.

You need to start thinking of your reputation as your brand because that's what it is; damage it and you damage your career.

You Put Your Reputation at Risk ❒ Guilty ❒ Not Guilty

Chapter 42 Adhere To The 80/20 Rule

You're way behind. It's 95/5 now.

The Pareto Principle, known as the 80/20 rule, is commonly used to describe how 20% of something (the vital few) is responsible for 80% of the result (the trivial many). For example, 20% of a company's sales force might produce 80% of its sales, or 80% of a company's revenue is generated by 20% of its clients.

This concept of uneven distribution, or disproportionate cause and effect, applies to many situations and relationships, and it served us well in the twentieth century.

However, in my observation, it's mathematically obsolete. The vital few are fewer, and the trivial many are greater. The relationship is more disproportionate than ever before.

Would you like me to prove it? I can't. Any more than the original 80/20 rule can be proven. After all, it's a concept—not a law.

Perhaps you, too, have observed the degeneration of competence, performance, reliability, empathy, service, attitude, quality, effort, and productivity, among other things. Nearly anything of significance is now driven by an even more vital few.

Your company cannot afford for you to be trivial. So, if it's 95/5 now, how can everyone in your company be in the vital 5%?

They can't.

But you can.

That's why you're reading this book—and why you must be the vital exception to the trivial rule.

You Adhere to the 80/20 Rule ☐ Guilty ☐ Not Guilty

Chapter 43 Lack A Moral Compass

You have a moral compass, but you don't always follow it. Instead, you adjust your morals to meet your needs.

You know you're not supposed to lie, cheat, steal, kill, be envious, greedy, and a few other things. Call them sins, commandments, principles, whatever. The Bible told me so. The Bible told you so.

Sometimes you shade the truth, get a little greedy, and push the boundaries of these honorable, time-tested codes. Nobody's perfect, but you need to be reminded of this.

This is me reminding you.

Start acting like the Sarbanes-Oxley Act was written for you. Like a clergyman, therapist, or those guys in compliance are steering your ship.

Whether you're driven by faith-based principles or good old-fashioned secular values, you must apply these principles to the workplace so your company can thrive.

Don't hide things. Take the ethical approach. Do the right thing.

Even if you don't have a conscience, your company does.

Your Moral Compass Is Broken   ❑ Guilty ❑ Not Guilty

Chapter 44 Put Things Off

I know. You were given a book on how to stop procrastinating but you haven't read it yet. Very funny. Wanna know what's not funny? Trying to cash a paycheck you aren't getting. Just ask anyone who's been there.

It wouldn't be so bad if you just moved something to the bottom of the pile, but you never seem to get to it...ever. It keeps migrating to another pile and a new bottom.

A decision you can't make.

A meeting you don't want to call or attend.

A task that's tedious, uninteresting, thankless, without reward.

Some things you can put off; most things you shouldn't. If you don't retrain this instinct, the next thing at the bottom of the pile will be you. Sometimes the root cause of procrastination is indirect and unintentional, as with overthinking. Sometimes it's pure indecision or inner conflict. You need to make a decision. You'll recover quickly—unless you're guilty of that too. (Don't worry we'll get to that in a minute.)

As much as you're a "get-it-done-now" person, you find ways to put things off, waiting for the precise moment when the stress that comes from putting it off further intersects with the least time needed to get it done.

Maybe you're the type that just isn't bothered by being late or generating subpar work. I hope you won't be bothered trying to cash that check you're not getting either.

Stop putting off your company's success. Right now. Seriously.

You Put Things Off ❏ Guilty ❏ Not Guilty

Chapter 45 Trust Your Instincts

The problem with that is, your instincts are wrong. Not all of them but too many to count.

If that weren't the case, this book wouldn't exist.

Just because you think or do something automatically doesn't make it the right response. When you practice something right, you get really good at it. Unfortunately, the same thing happens when you practice something wrong.

To clarify, instincts are innate or reflexive; in the case of behavior, biology aside, they can be acquired or modified through repetition. Intuition is that sixth sense, that instantaneous insight that comes from life experience, without inference or reason per se. Intuition you should almost always trust.

The problem is with your *instincts*. You need to retrain them— starting right now.

Not coincidentally, this entire collection of natural human behaviors, misguided as they are, is related to instincts—the wrong ones. These actions may be reflexive, but you must work vigilantly to evaluate whether or not you are making the right choices and moving in the right directions.

If there's anything resembling a secret in this book, it's that—taken together—your traits and behaviors are instincts to recognize, evaluate, and retrain.

You Trust Your Instincts ☐ Guilty ☐ Not Guilty

Chapter 46 Be Slow To Recover

Everyone makes mistakes. I don't think you'd argue this includes you. But you often fail to recover, and when you do, it's usually too late.

Do you even notice this?

The greats among us are not great because they don't screw up but because they recognize their mistakes and tend to them quickly.

They make adjustments, large and small, on an ongoing basis, correcting those they detect right away.

On a small, everyday scale, these are the little things that must be corrected. Bigger than leaving out a comma, smaller than locking your keys in the car.

On a larger scale, these are big picture course corrections related to strategy or decisions that require prompt redirection. Much of the time, how you get there is less important than how you get out.

You make tens of small, instant adjustments to your golf swing to improve it. Maybe you should do the same with your other weaknesses, whether thoughts or actions.

You're human and will always make mistakes. The good news is that, even at the speed of business today, there is time to recover. But you cannot afford to do nothing, or worse, continue ignoring your mistakes. Put another way, getting the rebound is as important as taking the shot, sometimes more so.

You're Slow to Recover   ❐ Guilty ❐ Not Guilty

Chapter 47 Rush To Judgment

You're so smart, quick, and intuitive that you can evaluate a person or situation instantly and accurately 95% of the time. Good for you.

Seriously? Wow, you're even dumber than I thought.

Resist your instinct to judge people, solutions, and circumstances too quickly or harshly. You might be right. You are probably wrong.

Your company (you know, the place that issues your paycheck) needs you to be right. And I don't mean hitting just over .500. Your average has to be much better than that.

Like most of the issues in this book, you'd do well to fix this problem in your personal life too. Rushing to judgment might be a good idea if you really think someone's in danger, but generally speaking, it's not smart—in the office or out.

You don't get all the facts and are in too much of a hurry. Don't do that.

You Rush to Judgment ☐ Guilty ☐ Not Guilty

Chapter 48 Yin When You Should Yang

And vice versa. By now, you should realize that it's all about balance and training your mind and instincts to find that place along the continuum where you can be most effective. Here are some examples of what you're doing wrong:

You fail to balance short and long term thinking.

You don't properly assess upside and downside.

You try to force things when you should just let go.

You get caught up in details and miss the big picture.

You fight change when you should embrace it.

You ask for permission instead of forgiveness.

You back out when you should move in.

You lose your composure rather than remain calm.

You work more when you should take a break.

There's a right time and a wrong time for everything. Your job is to consider the options in each direction—and then figure out exactly what to do and when to do it. Keep in mind that there are sometimes more than two directions or extremes to consider and balance.

Know where to fall to avoid falling short.

You Yin When You Should Yang ❐ Guilty ❐ Not Guilty

Chapter 49 Don't Follow Up

This one makes my blood boil. You're so guilty of this you should be locked in the supply closet and forced to eat the cafeteria special you can't quite make out.

Why is it so hard for you to get back to people promptly, respond to their phone calls, emails, and requests? Don't you want that from them? It doesn't have to be instant, just reasonably quick; use your judgment. But stop ignoring, forgetting, being distracted or just plain rude.

I know you're busy. If you weren't, I'd question why you were being paid. I know you're valuable. If you weren't, I'd wonder how you were still there.

But so are your coworkers, suppliers, clients—the whole world is busy and important. If you leave things untied, unfinished, or unattended at the speed of business today, you slow your company down. Not good.

If you only have the guts to change a few things about yourself, consider this one among them. You may find this resolution easier to carry out than you think.

Your company needs you to work hard, smart, clean, and fast. If you can't keep the wheels turning at maximum speed, at least keep them turning.

You Don't Follow Up ☐ Guilty ☐ Not Guilty

Chapter 50 Confuse Your Priorities

I'd like to close with something that shines a light on one of your biggest problems. It's your priorities: They're out of order. What's worse, you probably don't even realize it.

Of all the things you can do wrong, the one you can least afford is not to decide what's important and worth focusing on in the first place. Even if you're extremely smart and goal-oriented, chances are you squander more of your precious time than you care to admit.

Well, start admitting.

It's time to give that which you value the most, the kind of laser-like focus and unswerving commitment it deserves. Your health, family, quality of life, community, work, finances, personal time, and interests are just a few.

Life is tough, and life is short. You need to make the most of every minute, even if that means consciously downshifting or recharging for however long you need to.

You need to establish your priorities, guard them ferociously, and let nothing get in your way. You need to know what matters most, at home, at work, and at play. You need to be ruthless—not with people but with your time. There is only so much of you to go around.

The more consistent you act with your values, attitudes, interests, and beliefs, the better off your company will be, too. In other words, get your priorities straight.

Your Priorities Are Mixed Up ❑ Guilty ❑ Not Guilty

NOW WHAT?

Three Simple Steps

Time to revisit my questions to you at the outset: Which behaviors are you guilty of and what are you going to do about it? It is time now for you to perform your own surgery—mind surgery. It is up to you because you're the only one who's truly in control and can effect real change. Below are three steps to help get you started on your path of change. The process of managing these behaviors is simple, but it's not easy.

Step 1: Identify Intrusions

Collect all the behaviors you checked off as "guilty" and put them somewhere they can be readily accessed: your computer, a piece of paper, a notebook, whatever works. Don't think of this collection as Pandora's box, but rather a box of chocolates—a treasure of sorts. These golden opportunities just look like problems. You are now consciously aware of which intrusive behaviors you need to manage.

Step 2: Observe and Retrain Your Instincts

Next, you need to become more attuned to your thought process and actions, as well as how others react to you. This doesn't mean obsessing over every single thing you do; it just means being aware of your automatic behaviors—instincts—in the context of the issues you identified as being "guilty." In effect, you're making the unconscious conscious so you can catch yourself in the act, like telling yourself not to reach for that second piece of cake. The goal is to first reduce the degree and frequency of the behavior, then extinguish it entirely. You are now beginning to observe and retrain your instincts.

Step 3: Read, Share, Persist

In addition to recognizing your problems and monitoring your actions, read anything you can get your hands on to help you with each issue. Find others with whom you're comfortable sharing and exchanging ideas to help each other. You really can be your own workplace therapist if you are aware of your issues, focus on correcting them, and remain vigilant. And this book doesn't stop here; it continues online with recommendations, as you'll see below.

Where to Go from Here

I have done my best to tell you the truth. And while it often hurts, the truth is ultimately one of the best tools you can have to fuel your career, become more productive, and reach your potential. Think of this book and self-assessment as a pit stop to visit every so often on your way to that ever-moving finish line—faster, with fewer bumps, and to help make the ride more efficient and enjoyable.

If you discovered a handful of things you were doing to sabotage your career without even realizing it, and corrected even a few of them, wouldn't that be a good thing?

The accompanying website www.KillYourCompany.com will be recommending books, websites, and other resources to help you improve your weaknesses and retrain your instincts.

There will also be a forum where you can become part of the larger discussion online. You'll be able to connect, contribute, and collaborate with others who have something to offer. With your input and theirs, perhaps we can all become more productive and shorten the timeline between promotions.

Delusion. Denial. Ignorance. These are not your friends or valid excuses for failing to serve yourself and your company or association. Reality—now, that's a friend you can count on.

In Closing

None of us is perfect, and we can't expect to change overnight. So, chip away at it—one day at a time. You'll thank me later. Your company will thank you immediately. Even if it doesn't tell you, trust me, it will appreciate your efforts and likely reward you in time.

Oh, and thanks for reading. You don't suck at that.

www.KillYourCompany.com

CPSIA information can be obtained
at www.ICGtesting.com
Printed in the USA
FSOW01n0801300316
18623FS

9 781475 905267